LIBRARY SERVICES

http://e-library.eastsussexcc.gov.uk

East Sussex County Council

- Please return by the latest date below to avoid a charge.
- You may renew this item by phone, letter or on the website if it has not been requested by another reader. Please quote your ticket number and/or the number on the bar code label below.

Thank you for using your Library Service

CL 130

WELCOME TO MY COUNTRY

Welcome to
JAMAICA

FRANKLIN WATTS
LONDON•SYDNEY

This edition first published in 2005 by
Franklin Watts
96 Leonard Street
London EC2A 4XD

Franklin Watts Australia
45-51 Huntley Street
Alexandria NSW 2015

This edition is published for sale only in the United Kingdom & Eire.

© Marshall Cavendish International (Asia) Pte Ltd 2005
Originated and designed by Times Editions–Marshall Cavendish
an imprint of Marshall Cavendish International (Asia) Pte Ltd
A member of the Times Publishing Group
Times Centre, 1 New Industrial Road
Singapore 536196

Written by: Karen Kwek
Editor: Melvin Neo
Designer: Geoslyn Lim
Picture researcher: Susan Jane Manuel

A CIP catalogue record for this book
is available from the British Library.

ISBN 0 7496 6019 8

Printed in Singapore

Contents

Words that appear in the glossary are printed in **boldface** type the first time they occur in the text.

Welcome to Jamaica!

Jamaica is a small island located in the Caribbean Sea. The country is known for its sunny beaches and beautiful mountains, but it also has a history of hardship and struggle. Today, Jamaica has a **diverse** blend of **cultures**. Let's learn more about Jamaica and its people!

Opposite: Jamaica is a great place to enjoy the sea. These beach huts are in Negril, a resort area on the western edge of the island.

Below: A market in Jamaica sells handicrafts made by local people.

The Flag of Jamaica

The colour gold on the Jamaican flag symbolises wealth and sunlight. Black stands for strength and creativity. Green represents Jamaica's plentiful natural resources and the hope of its people.

The Land

Jamaica is part of the Greater Antilles, a chain of islands on the northern edge of the Caribbean Sea. The countries nearest to Jamaica are Cuba to the north and Haiti to the east.

The island of Jamaica has an area of 10,992 square kilometres. Jamaica is actually the tip of a mountain that lies mostly beneath the sea's surface. Much of the land consists of mountains and valleys.

Below: Montego Bay is one of Jamaica's main tourist centres.

Left: Many rare plants grow in the forests of the Blue Mountains. Jamaica's Blue coffee trees which produce the world-famous Jamaica Blue coffee beans also grow here.

The main mountain range in Jamaica extends east to west along the centre of the island. It is often called "the backbone of Jamaica". In the east lie the Blue Mountains and the John Crow Mountains. Dolphin Head, a proposed national park, is in the west.

Parks and Plantations

Jamaica has two national parks; the Blue Mountains-John Crow National Park and Montego Bay Marine Park. It also has many botanical gardens as well as sugar cane and fruit **plantations**.

Climate

Jamaica has a mostly warm climate, but temperatures on the island vary. In Kingston, Jamaica's capital, the annual average temperature is about 32° Celsius. At higher **altitudes** in the mountains, temperatures are cooler. The island has two rainy seasons, one in May and another during the months of October and November.

Above: The Rio Grande flows through eastern Jamaica. The island's largest **navigable** river is the Black River. Because Jamaica is so mountainous, most rivers are not navigable.

Plants and Animals

Jamaican plant life includes many species of orchids and ferns. The island's most common mammal is the mongoose. The **endangered** Jamaican hutia, or coney, is a mammal that looks like a guinea pig. Jamaica also has many species of bats, frogs, lizards and birds. The streamer tail hummingbird, the national bird, is also known to the locals as "Doctor Bird".

Below: Crocodiles can be found in wetlands and mangrove swamps on the southern coast of Jamaica. More than seven hundred species of fish live in the waters around the island.

History

Before the late 1400s, Jamaica was home to the native **Taino** people. Then in 1494, Christopher Columbus landed on the island. The Spanish built a **colony** there in 1509. They forced the Taino people to work as slaves on the plantations.

By the 1600s, European diseases, hard work and harsh treatment had wiped out most of the Taino people.

Left: Spanish Town was once the capital of Jamaica. Many of the government buildings in the city are built in the European style.

English Rule

In 1655, the English captured Jamaica from the Spanish. With most of the Taino people gone, the English used **indentured** plantation workers from other Caribbean islands and England. Later, slaves were brought from Africa. In 1838, slaves in Jamaica were freed, and workers were hired from countries such as China and India.

Left: A student stands next to a mural of Paul Bogle. A church leader who sought better conditions for his people, Bogle was made a national hero in 1969. This award is given to important people in the history of Jamaica.

The 1865 Rebellion

After slavery ended, conditions were very bad for Jamaica's black people. White people treated them unfairly. Sugar prices fell and many people lost their jobs on the plantations.

In 1865, farmer Paul Bogle led a group of peasants in a **rebellion** against Jamaica's white rulers. The group marched to the courthouse in Morant Bay where violence broke out. The courthouse caught fire and several people died. Paul Bogle was hanged for his part in the rebellion.

Political Changes

By the early 1900s, Jamaican workers were forming **trade unions**. Through these groups, workers could ask for higher **wages** and better working conditions. Political parties, such as the People's National Party (PNP) and the Jamaica Labour Party (JLP), were then created to fight for more say in how Jamaica was governed.

In 1944, all adult Jamaicans were given the right to vote. Elections were held that year, and the JLP won.

Below: In this 1962 photograph taken at Buckingham Palace in London, Britain's Queen Elizabeth II (*front row, middle*) poses with leaders from several nations. Alexander Bustamante, the prime minister of Jamaica at the time, stands directly behind the queen.

The Road to Independence

During and after World War II (1939–1945), Jamaicans continued to protest for more control of their government. Jamaica was still a British colony. In 1959, Jamaica was granted full self-government and PNP leader Norman Manley became prime minister. In 1962, Jamaica gained independence. That same year, Alexander Bustamante became the first prime minister of an independent Jamaica.

Below: Alexander Bustamante (*far left*) and Norman Manley (*far right*) shake hands with British officials after the Jamaica Independence Conference held in 1962.

Mary Jane Seacole (1805–1881)

A highly skilled nurse, Mary Jane Seacole learned traditional healing methods from her mother. When a disease called cholera broke out in the Caribbean islands in 1850, she prepared a cure. She spent her life caring for the sick and injured.

Mary Jane Seacole

Sir Alexander Bustamante (1884–1977)

The first prime minister of independent Jamaica, Alexander Bustamante established the first Jamaican trade union. He was made a national hero for his role in freeing Jamaica from British rule.

Sir Alexander Bustamante

Dr. Thomas P. Lecky (1904–1994)

Thomas Lecky is best known for creating Jamaica's own breed of cattle called the "Jamaica Hope". This popular breed produces more milk than other tropical breeds.

Government and the Economy

The Jamaican government is made up of the executive, legislative and judicial branches. The executive branch has a cabinet of ministers led by a prime minister who heads the government. The country's legislative branch, the **parliament**, consists of the Senate and the House of Representatives. It creates Jamaica's laws. A system of courts makes up the judicial branch.

Below:
This government building is located in Spanish Town. The city was the capital of Jamaica until 1872 when Kingston became the capital.

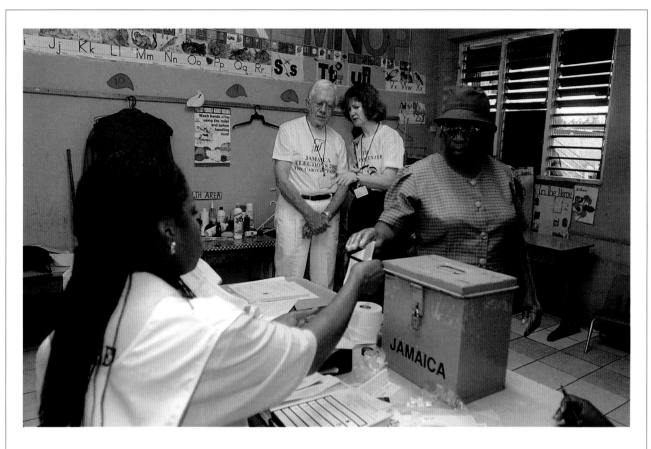

Local Government

Parish councils make up Jamaica's local government. Jamaica has three counties—Cornwall, Middlesex and Surrey—and it is also divided into fourteen parishes. Every parish is governed by a parish council that handles matters such as public health, garbage collection and maintenance of roads, parks and markets. The councils receive money from Jamaica's central government based in Kingston.

Above:
This woman is voting in the Jamaican general elections. Parish council members are elected every three years, and elections for the House of Representatives are held at least once every five years. All Jamaicans aged eighteen and older can vote.

Economy

The economy of Jamaica is healthy compared to other Caribbean nations. However, Jamaicans do suffer from rising prices and a shortage of jobs.

Jamaica's main industries include tourism, agriculture and mining. A large number of Jamaicans work in tourism-related jobs. The country's main crops are sugar cane, bananas, citrus fruits, coffee, coconuts and **pimento** (allspice). Mines in Jamaica produce bauxite, a substance that is used to make the metal aluminium.

Above: Young banana plants are carefully grown at this nursery. Most of the banana plantations in Jamaica are on the eastern side of the island.

Left: Formed in 1969, Air Jamaica plays a key role in the Jamaican tourist industry. Tourism is an important part of Jamaica's economy.

Trade

Jamaica trades mainly with the United States, Canada, the United Kingdom and other European nations. The country's **imports** include finished goods and raw materials. Its **exports** include crops and bauxite.

Getting Around

Most people travel around Jamaica by car, bus or aeroplane. The island has two international airports and four domestic or local airports.

Above: Buses are a common form of transportation in Jamaica.

19

People and Lifestyle

Jamaicans are **descendants** of people from many different cultures. Before slavery ended in 1838, West African slaves and Europeans came to the island. After 1838, Chinese, East Indians and more Europeans arrived.

Today, Jamaica has a population of more than 2.7 million people. At least another 2 million Jamaicans live in other countries all over the world.

Below:
Many people visit the markets along the streets of Montego Bay.

Jamaica's motto—"Out of Many, One People"—describes the way different kinds of people live together in Jamaica, creating a unique blend of cultures. More than 90 per cent of Jamaicans are of African descent and 7.3 per cent are of mixed parentage. The island is also home to East Indians, Chinese, Jews and whites descended from European indentured workers.

Above: Children of different races study and play together every day in Jamaica. The **constitution** of Jamaica gives all racial groups the same rights.

City and Country Living

Kingston is the capital of Jamaica. It is the centre of government, business and culture on the island, and it is steadily growing. Many people live in Kingston. Others travel there every day to work.

In the countryside, many families are extremely poor. Most people work on farms. They may own their own farms or work on other people's farms. Some people have jobs in mining or tourism.

Below:
This shack is in Cockpit Country. Some parts of the Jamaican countryside do not have proper housing, schools or public services.

Family Life

Jamaica has many kinds of families. Some families consist of two parents and children, while others consist of one parent and children. In recent years, the number of single mothers has risen. Jamaica also has extended families, with parents, children and other relatives living together. Many parents go to the United States and England to find work, leaving their children with relatives or guardians.

Above: Families in Jamaica often spend Sundays together at home after they return from church. On the island, most fathers play a smaller role in raising children than mothers do.

Education

In the past, few Jamaicans received a decent education. Today, 88 per cent of Jamaicans aged fifteen and older can read and write.

Children in Jamaica start school at age three. They usually spend two years in nursery school and six years in primary school. They attend high school for five years. Some students continue their education at one of the universities on the island.

Below: These Jamaican primary-school students are enjoying a recess break. In Jamaica, students begin high school at age eleven or twelve.

Women in Jamaica

Women play many important roles in Jamaica. Most Jamaican women are very independent, and many of them are single mothers who must support their families. Although the Jamaican government does not have many women leaders, more women than men work in Jamaica. Most of the country's teachers are women. A high percentage of women in Jamaica can read and write, and more women than men attend Jamaica's universities.

Above: In Jamaica, women are an important part of the workforce.

Below: This woman in Jamaica sells flowers and fruit.

Religion

Christianity came to Jamaica in the 1500s when the Spanish introduced Roman Catholicism. Later, the English brought **Protestant** beliefs. Today, more than 65 per cent of Jamaicans are Christian, and most of these Christians are Protestants. The Church of God is the largest Protestant group. Other Protestant groups include Baptists, Anglicans, Seventh-Day Adventists and Pentecostalists.

Below: North Street Cathedral in Kingston is one of many churches in Jamaica. Churches are centres of social life in Jamaican communities.

Left: A Kumina priestess moves to drumbeats and chanting. Followers of Kumina believe spirits can be found in natural objects such as trees and rocks, and that these spirits can be persuaded to do good or evil.

Below: Haile Selassie was the ruler of Ethiopia, an African country. Followers of Rastafarianism, which began in Jamaica, believe that Selassie is a saviour of black people and the king of all Africa.

Almost 35 per cent of Jamaicans are followers of non-Christian religions, which include Judaism, Islam, Hinduism, Rastafarianism and traditional African beliefs. *Pocomania* and *Kumina* are traditional Jamaican religions that have African roots.

Language

The official language of Jamaica is English. In everyday conversation however, many people in Jamaica speak Jamaican *patois*. This patois is a mixture of Creole English (spoken by the British settlers in Jamaica), the African languages of slaves and Spanish and Portuguese words. Schools in Jamaica used to discourage students from using this patois but it is now recognised as the country's second language.

Below:
Most Jamaican newspapers and official documents as well as many books are written in standard British English. However, Jamaican patois is more widely spoken than standard English.

Literature

Jamaican literature began to **flourish** in the 1960s when Jamaica gained independence. Some Jamaicans wrote about the problems of British rule, including slavery. Other Jamaicans, such as Louise Bennett-Coverley, wrote about everyday life on the island. Coverley and other writers also explored the use of Jamaican patois, helping it to become better accepted by the people in Jamaica.

Above: In Jamaican schools, students read the works of many Jamaican writers. These works include the poems and stories of Louise Bennett-Coverley who is known as "Miss Lou".

Arts

Jamaica has a wide variety of arts, including music, dance, drama and visual arts. The National Gallery in Kingston is a good place to explore the country's visual arts. It houses Jamaica's largest collection of historical and contemporary art and features the works of many well-known Jamaican sculptors, painters and potters.

Pottery is the oldest of Jamaican arts. The island's first potters were the native Taino people who used red clay to make cooking pots and other items.

Above: A potter works on his latest creation.

Left: The National Gallery in Kingston displays the works of many well-known Jamaican artists, such as potter Cecil Baugh and sculptor Edna Manley.

Dance

Jamaicans love to dance. Traditional dance forms in Jamaica have strong African roots. They include Myal, Revival, Quadrille and Maypole. Modern Jamaican dance is a mixture of traditional dance forms, European classical ballet and modern dance styles from the United States. The most important dance company in the country is the National Dance Theatre Company.

Above:
In Jamaica, dances are often performed for tourists. These dances showcase the rich history of dance on the island.

Theatre

Jamaican theatre groups perform a wide range of works. Many performances mix standard theatrical forms, such as drama and comedy, with the acting, singing and dancing of Jamaican folk theatre. Performances also combine standard English and Jamaican patois.

Some theatre groups, such as the ASHE Performing Arts Ensemble, use the performing arts to address social problems in Jamaica. This ensemble mostly consists of young Jamaicans.

Below: Kingston's Ward Theatre is a well-known playhouse in Jamaica. Many theatre groups are based in Kingston.

Music

Jamaica has traditional and popular styles of music. Traditional music has roots in the folk music of African slaves. It is often played on special occasions. Reggae is the most famous popular music in Jamaica. It followed other popular styles, such as mento, ska and rock steady. In the 1970s, reggae musicians such as Bob Marley began having international success. A form of reggae called dancehall is now popular with young Jamaicans.

Below: Jamaican reggae star Bob Marley made fans around the world with his unique music. He often sang about hope and freedom. He died in 1981.

Leisure

Jamaicans like to spend their free time in groups—the bigger, the better! They enjoy sports and games such as dominoes. Jamaicans also like to go to music festivals. Reggae Sumfest is one of the most exciting music festivals on the island. Every year, it brings together reggae fans from Jamaica and many other parts of the world.

Below: These young Jamaicans are enjoying a day in Kingston. From shopping malls to cinemas to the most popular dance clubs, Kingston's many attractions draw crowds of young people to the city.

Many Jamaicans enjoy going to the movies. Sometimes, they may see their own country on the screen, because Jamaica is a favourite setting for filmmakers. Several local movies have been made in Jamaica. The first Jamaican-made movie seen by audiences worldwide was *The Harder They Come* in 1973. It stars Jamaican musician Jimmy Cliff and is famous for its reggae soundtrack.

Above: Jamaican-born actress Grace Jones (*far right*) starred with Tanya Roberts (*far left*) and Roger Moore (*centre*) in the 1985 James Bond film *A View to a Kill*.

Sports

Sports are a big part of leisure in Jamaica. Soccer, cricket, basketball and netball are popular sports on the island. The Jamaican women's netball team is ranked one of the best in the world. In 1998, the national soccer team reached the World Cup finals for the first time. Jamaicans also like to watch horse racing.

Below: Jamaicans of all ages enjoy beach soccer.

Jamaican Champions

Jamaican athletes have excelled at track-and-field, becoming Olympic medalists and world champions. At the 1980 Olympic Games, sprinter Merlene Ottey became the first Jamaican female athlete to win an Olympic medal. More recently, Greg Haughton won two bronze medals for Jamaica at the 2000 Olympic Games.

Above: *The Athlete*, a sculpture by Alvin Marriott, stands near the National Stadium in Kingston.

Holidays and Festivals

Jamaica has ten public holidays each year, including Christian holidays such as Christmas and Easter. The island also has several festivals.

Emancipation Day is the first day of August. This holiday marks the date when slaves in Jamaica were officially freed. Independence Day on 6 August marks the date when Jamaica became an independent nation.

Below: These local women are performing a folk dance as part of Independence Day celebrations in Jamaica.

The Jamaica Festival is a mixture of exhibitions and competitions in music, dance and other arts. Held in summer, the festival takes place throughout the island. Thousands of Jamaicans of all ages help prepare for the festival.

National Heritage Week is held in October and includes National Heroes Day, a public holiday. Events during the week celebrate Jamaican culture and the achievements of Jamaicans.

Above: In Jamaica, holidays are a time when many families relax together at home.

Food

Traditional Jamaican food uses a lot of seasonings, including salt, black pepper, pimento, garlic, onions and hot peppers. The national dish, ackee and saltfish, combines ackee, a fruit, with heavily salted cod. It is usually a breakfast dish and is often served on Sundays with other foods, such as yams or dumplings. Other traditional foods are hardough (a heavy, white bread) and fried bammies (flat cakes made from **cassava**).

Left: The bright red ackee fruit is poisonous when unripe. When ripe, the fruit opens up. The yellow flesh inside can then be cooked and eaten.

Jerk meat is another Jamaican food. This dish is made from pork, chicken or fish. First, the meat is **marinated** in herbs and spices. Then it is wrapped in leaves and slowly cooked over a fire of pimento wood. Jamaican jerk meat is also sold in other countries.

The dishes of other cultures can also be found in Jamaica. Chinese and East Indian workers brought their own foods, cooking styles and seasonings to the island. The East Indians, for example, introduced a dish called curry goat that is very popular.

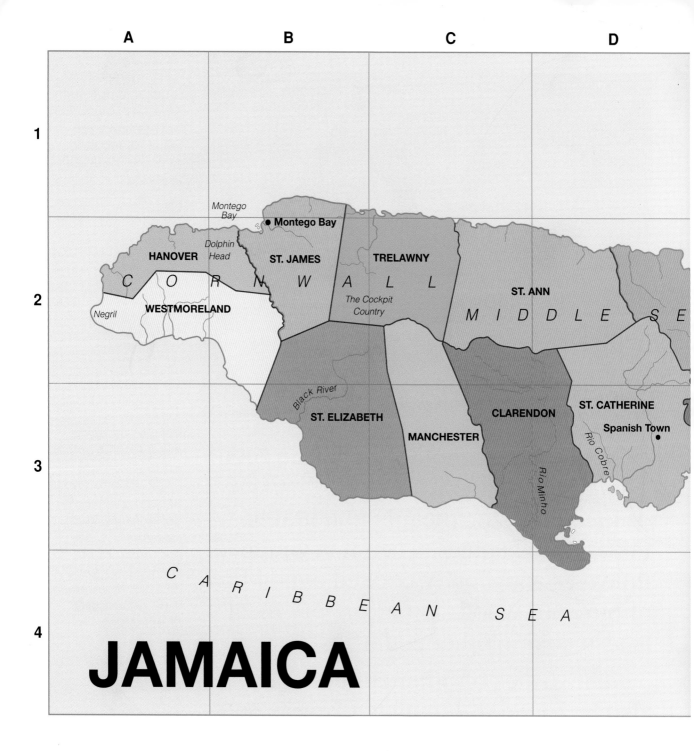

JAMAICA

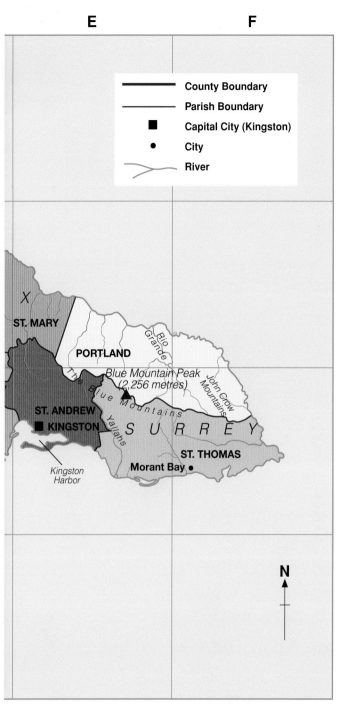

Black River B2–B3	**Middlesex** C2–D3
	Montego Bay B2
Blue Mountain Peak E3	**Morant Bay** F3
Blue Mountains E3–F3	**Negril** A2
Caribbean Sea A4–F4	**Portland** E2–F3
Clarendon C2–D4	**Rio Grande** E2–F3
Cockpit Country B2–C3	**Rio Cobre** D3
Cornwall A2–C3	**St. Andrew** D2–E3
	St. Ann C2–D2
Dolphin Head B2	**St. Catherine** D2–D3
	St. Elizabeth B2–C3
Hanover A2–B2	**St. James** B1–B2
	St. Mary D2–E2
John Crow Mountains F3	**St. Thomas** E3–F3
	Spanish Town D3
Kingston E3	**Surrey** E2–F3
Kingston Harbor D3–E3	**Trelawny** B1–C2
Manchester C2–C3	**Westmoreland** A2–B3

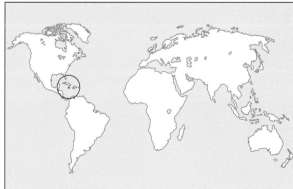

Quick Facts

Official Name	Jamaica
Capital	Kingston
Main Languages	English (official), Jamaican patois
Population	2,713,130 (July 2004 estimate)
Land Area	10,992 square km
Counties	Cornwall, Middlesex, Surrey
Parishes	Clarendon, Hanover, Kingston, Manchester, Portland, St. Andrew, St. Ann, St. Catherine, St. Elizabeth, St. James, St. Mary, St. Thomas, Trelawny, Westmoreland
Highest Point	Blue Mountain Peak 2,256 metres
Major Rivers	Black River, Rio Cobre, Rio Grande
Main Religion	Christianity
Major Holidays	Good Friday (March/April) Easter (March/April) Emancipation Day (1 August) Independence Day (6 August) Christmas (25 December)
Currency	Jamaican Dollar (JMD 110.904 = £1 in June 2004)

Opposite: The white egret is one of many bird species found in Jamaica.

Glossary

altitudes: heights above sea level.

cassava: a kind of plant with a root that can be cooked and eaten.

colony: an area that is settled and governed by another country.

constitution: a set of laws establishing how a country is governed and the rights of the people.

cultures: the sets of customs, beliefs, language, literature and art belonging to particular peoples or countries.

descendants: the later generations of particular families.

diverse: having many differences and much variety.

endangered: in danger of dying out completely or becoming extinct.

exports: goods sent out of a country to be sold in another country.

flourish: grow or develop quickly and successfully.

imports: goods from other countries that are brought into a country to be sold there.

indentured: having signed an agreement to work for a person for a period of time, often in return for the payment of transportation and other costs.

marinated: soaked in something, such as seasonings, before being cooked.

navigable: suitable for travel by boat.

parliament: an official government body of elected representatives who make the laws of their country.

patois: the special language of a certain group of people.

pimento: the berry of the pimento tree, which is often dried and used as a seasoning, also called allspice.

plantations: large farms which usually have many workers.

Protestant: part of a particular group of Christian faiths that differ from Roman Catholicism.

rebellion: organised opposition to a government or other authority.

Taino: the native people of islands in the Caribbean Sea.

trade unions: organisations of workers that try to improve wages, benefits and working conditions for members.

wages: the money workers receive.

More Books to Read

Caribbean New Wave, Contemporary Short Stories. Stewart Brown (Heinemann Library)

It Begins With Tears. Caribbean Writers series. Opal Palmer Adisa (Heinemann Library)

Jamaica. Letters from Around the World series. Ali Brownlie (Evans Publishing Group)

Jamaica. Living In series. Judy Bastyra (Franklin Watts)

Jamaica. Picture a Country series. Henry Pluckrose (Franklin Watts)

Stone Haven. Caribbean Writers Series. Evan Jones (Heinemann Library)

We Come from: Jamaica. Alison Brownlie (Hodder Wayland)

What's It Like to Live In: Jamaica? Alison Brownlie (Hodder Wayland)

Videos

Jamaica – Land of Food and Water (Ivn Entertainment)

Lonely Planet: Jamaica – The Experience (Ivn Entertainment)

Web Sites

http://nature.org/wherewework/caribbean/jamaica

www.elmuseo.org/taino

www.jnht.com

www.nlj.org.jm/docs/heroes_emblems.htm

Due to the dynamic nature of the Internet, some web sites stay current longer than others. To find additional web sites, use a reliable search engine with one or more of the following keywords to help you locate information about Jamaica. *Bob Marley, dancehall music, John Crow Mountains, Kingston, reggae, Spanish Town, Taino.*

Note to parents and teachers
Every effort has been made by the Publishers to ensure that these web sites are suitable for children; that they are of the highest educational value, and that they contain no inappropriate or offensive material. However, because of the nature of the Internet, it is impossible to guarantee that the contents of these sites will not be altered. We strongly advise that Internet access is supervised by a responsible adult.

Index